TUG-O-WAR TEENS
NO INVITATION TO A DESTINATION

SEPTIMUS BARROCK

Library of Congress Control Number: 2024923237

ISBN: 979-8-3306-1786-9   (Paperback)
ISBN: 979-8-3306-1787-6   (eBook)

Printed in the United States of America

CONTENTS

FOREWORD

By
TASHA FALCONER

The teenage years are filled with bliss and wonder and irrationality and misperceptions and risk-taking and…fill in the blanks with all kinds of maladaptation, but they are also filled with fun and energy and hope and promise. The teenagers of today will grow up to be the leaders and innovators and movers and shakers of the future so it is incumbent on society to give them a break and guide them to places where they could fulfill those roles. The foregoing statements are commensurate with what could be considered 'normal teenager dispositions', but when the element of neglect, lack of guidance, lack of love, and a general lack of ability to meet basic needs are thrown into the mix, the resulting product is a troubled teen who still has to function within the norms of society.

In his book Tug-O-War Teens, Septimus Barrock narrates episodes of behaviors he observed as a teacher at an alternative high school for juvenile offenders. The author not only reports on the behaviors themselves, but also employs compassion as he endeavors to understand what the catalysts for the behaviors are. Although much of the account will evoke a measure of disbelief in the reader, the author encourages empathy for the situations and circumstances the students find themselves in. The text is not all about doom and gloom. There are also bright spots that portend hopefulness.

When people are given opportunities to make progress in life there is never a guarantee that all of the recipients of those opportunities will make good use of them. Some will take those opportunities and use them to create even better opportunities for themselves, and some will squander those opportunities and maintain a posture of stagnation, but not to have given them that choice is to condemn them to an existence of failure. Tug-O-War Teens is a must read for anyone who can appreciate what troubled kids and the staff who work with them deal with on a daily basis.

In a world where survival often outweighs morality, the characters in this story navigate a reality marked by crime, struggle, and fleeting moments of hope. Set against the backdrop of an alternative school and the rough streets of Jacksonville, this tale takes you deep into the lives of students who have been dealt harsh circumstances but are still trying to find their way. As the narrator reflects on their experiences as a teacher, mentor, and sometimes witness to the darker side of society, you will encounter moments of despair, resilience, and unexpected humanity. The story unfolds with gritty realism, offering a raw look at the forces shaping these young lives—and the fragile line between redemption and destruction.

"As a veteran educator, I am deeply moved by how Septimus Barrock brings the real-life stories of Tug-O-War Teens to life. This book isn't just for teachers—it's for anyone with a heart. It grabs hold of your emotions and forces you to reflect, not only on the lives of these troubled teens but on your own capacity for empathy and understanding. A compelling, must-read that will resonate with you long after the final page."

BRYAN JOHNSON

CHAPTER ONE

THE FIRST PICK UP

The two riders on the van did not seem to be overly alarmed, but this was a surreal experience for me. This type of sight had only been familiar to me during my movie-going days and in the gangster movies I tended to enjoy. Upon pulling up to Roland's house, one of the passengers commented, 'That Nigga house been shot up!" I had gotten used to this kind of expression even though it pains me to hear these young people refer to each other in this derogatory fashion but also being aware that for them it is a term of endearment or ubiquitous greeting.

He uttered the comment in a kind of nonchalant way, but when I looked out of the window, I saw that the front of the house was bullet-ridden. Bullet holes decorated the outside walls of what looked to be a bedroom and living room area. It was a small house in a low-income neighborhood (emphasize *hood*) where residents struggled to make a living while navigating the desperation that had come to represent their lives.

I blew the horn to alert Roland that we were here to pick him up for school, but he was a no-show on that day. No-shows were not unusual because students, for one reason or another, would just not be in the mood to come to school at times. Later I would learn that their absences could be due to anything ranging from having not slept the night before, being sick, or not having clean clothes to wear. Many thoughts occupied my head as I observed *the scene of the crime* while waiting to see if Roland would come out.

I was wondering what he thought about having this type of activity targeting his household and whom he had 'beef' with that could expose his mom and other family members to bodily harm or even death! In the meantime, one of the passengers started talking about how several of his 'dead dogs' had met their demise as a result of drive-by shootings. By this time, I had driven away from Roland's house on my way to the next stop, but fascinated to listen to my passenger's account of his movie-like existence. He went on to explain the circumstances that led to his friends' *(dead dogs)* deaths. He said that the conflicts *('beefs')* were mainly about turf wars, youths responding to disrespectful lyrics published on Instagram by wannabe rappers, and issues regarding females.

I had worked as a teacher at an alternative school, and I was new to the area at that time. The staff at the school would be scheduled to do pick-ups and drop-offs in addition to their primary functions as teachers, mental health professionals, career advisors, administrators, behavior interventionists or case managers. We all wore several hats, but we banded together to make the system work. It was not the first time I had worked with this demographic of students. I had an assignment at a similar school in Miami thirteen years ago. That assignment lasted three years, but one operational difference was that the staff did not have to do pick-ups or drop-offs. The Miami operation was on a much larger scale, and the students arrived and departed on school buses.

In the most recent assignment, I recall how vulnerable I felt going into the 'hood' sometimes before sunrise to pick up students when I was new to the place and aware of some of the activities that go on in these areas; as told by the students themselves and sometimes reported in the news media. Some of the crimes in the media reports had been committed by perpetrators that some of the students knew, or even done by some of the students themselves. The school was located in a large city and a typical round trip from the school and back again would take two hours. Students were spread out over a large geographical area, and if traffic was not favorable, the time could extend beyond two hours.

Not all of the students lived in the hood, and not all of the students were from ethnic minority groups. What was common was that they were all referred to the program, by the Court, because of varying degrees of crimes they had committed; some violent with the use of firearms and some non-violent such as shoplifting or credit card fraud. They were all juveniles and at a stage of their lives where they lacked rational perspectives on many issues but were easily enticed and driven by wants and sometimes even needs. The inability to meet basic needs often undergirds the desperation to fill those needs, and whereas people who have a sense of patient morality will find a non-criminal way to meet those needs, others could deem it a matter of urgency to fulfill that need even if it means victimizing innocent people in order to do so.

I developed a strong rapport with most of the students, and they often confided in me about their concerns and the struggles they had faced. One common theme among them was their ambition to "get money." Whenever I asked, "How do you plan to get money?" the response was invariably the same: "Get money!" Sometimes, I overheard conversations where they casually mentioned breaking into houses or cars, stealing valuables like guns and jewelry, and selling them. Others spoke about dealing drugs.

It was clear that they understood the consequences of getting caught, especially while still in the program. They could be sent to juvenile detention for a period of time, or, in more severe cases, transferred to a higher-level program where their freedoms were significantly restricted. However, one punishment I found particularly disturbing was the permanent scars left on some of them by police K-9 dogs. When pursued and caught, officers sometimes allowed these dogs to bite the youth, leaving both physical and emotional wounds.

This practice harks back to a painful chapter in history, where dogs were used to suppress individuals involved in what was sometimes "good trouble." For these young offenders, being pursued and apprehended by police, this punishment seems not only excessive but also unevenly applied. This raises concerns about its true intent. Rather than guiding these youth toward reform and helping them grow into better individuals, such harsh measures dehumanize them. The physical and psychological scars left by these incidents may push them further down a destructive path, potentially setting them up as future candidates for the prison system.

Our program was a level 2, non-residential day program, and I had known of past students who continued to offend after they had left us and went on to serve extensive juvenile sentences in residential programs. The ones who complied with the program's rules and expectations could be done within four months, but I had seen some of them stay for up to one year because of poor attendance or failure to pass a drug test. The average time spent seemed to be around six to eight months; all because they were not disciplined enough to follow rules.

A few of the students had told me that they were just having a hard time quitting when it came to drug use. Most of them smoked marijuana, but some had indulged in the use of more potent drugs. One of them even said, "I can't stop smoking weed"! I would remind him that being clean for thirty days before a drug test was a requirement and a precondition for his release. Another one told me he started smoking weed when he was seven years old. I asked him how he was able to gain access to weed at such a young age, and he replied. "My mom gave it to me to smoke". Another youth told me that she regularly smoked marijuana with her dad.

On occasion, a few of them would test positive for other substances even though marijuana seemed to be the drug of choice. It would be easy to judge these kids and their parents, but generations of dysfunction underlie these vices. I have had kids tell me about their mothers being prostitutes, their fathers being drug dealers, their mothers wearing jewelry that the kids themselves broke into houses and stole, doing cocaine with her mother, and one kid even told me that his father once shot at him with a gun. How does one give hope to kids whose lives have been one predicament after another? The answer is: Don't give up on them! Even though all of them may not be able to be saved, give them hope, and let them decide what they want to do with it. But to simply walk away from them would be tantamount to complicity with those heartless people who have already decided these youngsters' fates for them.

CHAPTER TWO

PRISON LIFE

The system is not necessarily there to drill down on the vagaries that created these kids in the first place and does not appear to make a serious effort to find ways to turn them into productive adults. Kids like these seem too numerous to merit society's resolve to provide the individual attention they need, so the next stop in their troubled lives is likely to be jail or prison; perhaps because this latter step seems to be easier to implement. I will not go into a whole political discourse here, but this state of misery is not completely unembraced by all stakeholders. No one will cry over these 'throwaways'; especially not the corporations who run private prisons. Quite often I would give the kids pep talks about prison life. I gave them the truth about what they would be likely to face if they ended up in such a place.

I knew that my co-workers and I were not the only ones who talked to them about choosing another way. I am sure many of their family members told them about being in this situation of neo-slavery, but because some of those family members are themselves repeat offenders, they may have been looked upon as dubious messengers and unwitting conditioners of what the minds of their children or siblings could have perceived as a necessary path to travel. If going to jail is seen as just another part of these youths' experience, then they may be condemned to carry on the tradition.

When I talked to them about this topic, they initially looked at me as an unlikely spokesperson for this type of message given my clean disposition, education and dogged conformity to decency. They would ask me, disbelievingly, if I had been to prison and what I could possibly have done to land me there. It was at this point when I would play a little mind game with them and declare that I didn't want to speak about it. On occasion, one or two of them would ask me if I had ever been in the military and if I had ever killed anyone. Here again I would tell them that I would leave it up to them to figure it out. They would make mention of the way I walked and the way I talked, and even how strong I looked. They would also ask me if I worked out.

When I told them I did one hundred incline pushups daily they found it hard to believe, but that part was true. That was not banter designed to keep them in wonderment. Between five and six every morning I would do my exercise routine which involved pushups and stretches. This kept me alert and energized every day. I suppose a certain degree of doubt is in order when a sixty-seven-year-old man claims to have the ability to perform such a feat while his sixteen and seventeen-year-old students cannot do it. At that age they are full of energy, and one or two of them had even tried to do incline pushups in the classroom only to quit after between ten and fifteen reps.

I had not accepted their invitation to perform proof of my ability to do a hundred, but I had it in mind just to do it spontaneously for them one day. During my time at the Miami school, thirteen years ago, I routinely did sixty pushups every morning. A strong air of doubt also existed with those students then, but I put their thinking to rest by one day impulsively doing sixty incline pushups for them to see. Back to the pep talks I would give my recent students: I would often relate some of the firsthand experiences I had had over the eight and a half months I spent at a maximum security prison, and some of the stories related by inmates.

I would let them know about the element of total control they would be subjected to; when to sleep, when to eat, where to walk, when to walk, etc. The high probability of being raped as a young person entering the institution is real. I recall one inmate telling me that he had to intervene as two other inmates were in the process of raping an eighteen-year-old young man who had just arrived at the prison. Of course my students would tell me that they would never allow anyone to rape them in prison. I would ask them how they would avoid it, and they would say that it just would not happen. My retort would always be that they should avoid going to prison in the first place and there would not be any need to face that situation.

The next thing about prison is the violence that can erupt at any time. There is a myriad of physical and emotional realities. I once saw two inmates embracing and weeping bitterly. When I inquired, I learned that one of them was distraught because his boyfriend had been stabbed in the face that morning. Apparently there was some sort of love triangle which caused a measure of jealousy that escalated to violence. I also learned about inmates making homemade (prison-made) wine by pouring orange juice into the toilet bowl and leaving it there for a period of time until it fermented. In the meantime, someone had the duty of guarding the toilet bowl so that it would not be used until the process was complete and the wine removed from that receptacle.

I would tell them that I would observe lifers shaking nervously as they sat in deep contemplation. Some inmates have had their mothers, or other family members, transition from this life, and this became a source of great frustration seeing that they were not able to attend the funeral. Others have told me about the grandchildren they would never get to see or the wives or girlfriends that have moved on with their lives. One day I saw the frustration on a lifer's face. When I asked him what was going on, he told me that he found out that his best friend had been having sex with his fiancé while he, the lifer, is in prison. Most of the inmates would rather be on the outside living normal lives. They talk about having relationships on the outside and fantasizing about being physically able to be next to the person they love. But none of this would materialize given their sentence of "life without the possibility of parole"

I would sometimes look on their records to see what I could learn about these inmates' reasons for being perpetually confined to the prison walls. It's so interesting to observe the paradox associated with this prison life. It's almost comical to see how it is noted on the inmates' record what their earliest release date would be. Most of them looked so unassuming, but to see an earliest release date listed as the year 2044 or 9999 is quite bizarre. Nonetheless, this is the state of affairs that exists with these prisoners. An inmate who is thirty years old and has an earliest release date of 2044 has hopes of being on the outside one day. The inmate who has an earliest release date of 9999 has hopes as well; but he is just not going to live long enough to walk out of the institution.

From what I had seen, all of the inmates have expectations of walking free one day. That is perhaps why the prison library is the busiest part of the compound. Inmates go there to research landmark cases to see if they could discover any loopholes; anything they could use to get a new trial. I had not seen any of them successfully launch a petition for a retrial during the time I was there, but I have heard some of them make mention of reasons why they were wrongly convicted. In all instances, they claim that it was a case of mistaken identity. One told me he told the authorities he knows who the real culprit is, but just happened to be in the wrong place at the wrong time. Another one said that dead bodies were being found after he had been arrested, indicating that the true killer continued his killing spree while the inmate was already off of the streets.

I relayed these accounts to my juvenile students in the hope that they would see no upside to being in the prison environment. My stint as a GED instructor at that maximum security prison was nothing less than an education for me. I am hopeful there is the probability that my reporting would serve to convince some of my recent students to cease their criminal behavior - but perhaps, they might not be convinced at all. In a few instances, students have committed serious enough offenses to land them in jail.

On the evening news, I saw a report of a youth who shot another youth in a dispute over a girl. I recognized the picture and name of the shooter. It was De'Cray, one of my students with whom I had a good rapport. He had a pleasant disposition, and always endeavored to do his classwork even though it was a struggle for him to achieve passing grades. He was one of the students who had taken an unnecessary hiatus from attending regular school, or any school for that matter. De'Cray never showed me any disrespect, and would laugh at my not-always-funny jokes. As an aside, I bill myself as a teacher/entertainer who has tried out his fantasy stand-up comedy routines on his captive audience, his students, sometimes with resulting sarcastic laughs and/or boos.

CHAPTER THREE

ON THE VAN

I have to say that one of the times of heightened concern for a staff/ driver is when the students are on the van. I remember once feeling quite nervous when I observed a student making obscene gestures to a motorist. I was eventually able to assert that there should be no gesturing, calling, or waving to motorists when on the van. The students thought I was being a little extreme, but in spite of their obliviousness to my thinking, or the potential dangers posed by their behavior, I had zero appetite for being a victim of road rage. Return trips in the evenings were especially prone to aberrant behaviors by students. In the morning the youths tend to be a little groggy from lack of sleep the night before. Listening to them talk when they came to class, I surmised that sometimes they are on the streets late at night, playing video games late into the night, texting or talking on the phone or just having a bout with insomnia.

On the trip back to their' houses, they replay the events of the day, and on occasion unwittingly say something unflattering about someone on the van. Arguments, abusive language and threats could erupt over the silliest things. For the most part the youths would stop the behavior in response to the staff's demand, but sometimes the driver is left with no choice but to stop the van and threaten to put the offenders off or even return to the school and call the parents to pick the students up depending on the severity of the situation. There is also the option to call the police if it is determined that the situation warrants it, but sometimes other circumstances unfold.

One time after the school day had ended I was driving home because I was not scheduled to do drop-offs on that day. I looked in my rearview mirror and noticed one of the school's vans in the lane next to me. Mr. Tomorrow, a fellow teacher, was the driver. The students he was transporting recognized my vehicle and some of them made gestures to me; merely waving and making faces, but surprisingly nothing obscene. I thought it kind of noteworthy when Mr. Tomorrow went into the turning lane and made a U-Turn heading back in the direction of the school. My instincts told me that something was up, so I made a U-Turn as well and drove towards the school.

The van made it there before me, but I had a clear view of the parking lot where Mr. Tomorrow had pulled up as I waited for the oncoming traffic to clear. Mr. Cobbler, Ms. Stefan, and Mr. Roko, all senior personnel, were waiting for the arrival of the van. I could see Ms. Stefan escorting Matte, a student who was on the van, away from the area. Matte was only halfway compliant at first, but he relented and walked away at Ms. Stefan's direction. Mr. Cobbler and Mr. Roko concentrated on ensuring there was order among the remaining students on the van.

I had a notion about the genesis of the situation that caused Mr. Tomorrow to go back to the school. Tension had been brewing between Matte and another student, Torey over a pair of shoes that Matte had traded with Torey while she took a trip out of state. The idea was, I came to understand, for the two students to do a mutual return of the shoes once Torey came back from her trip. For some reason, Torey did not do a timely re-trade, and this escalated to a near fight between the two in the cafeteria. Vigilant staff noticed a physical squaring off between Matte and Torey and intervened to separate them.

In the classroom, I observed chatter by other students about the situation, as Torey would give her take and Matte would give his take as well. Matte and Torey were not in the same class, but they rotated among classes during the school day. Unfortunately, they rode the same van to and from school because they lived on the same route assigned to that van. This arrangement reeked of volatility so it was not altogether unexpected that something adverse could arise from the circumstance. Mr. Roko and Mr. Cobbler appeared to have helped Torey to temper her aggression, but I showed up in time to offer to take Matte home.

On the way, he gave me his version of the events but I just listened and did not give an opinion. The following day I was given a more extensive report about what transpired on Mr. Tomorrow's van the evening before. Matt and Torey began to argue over the shoes in question and in Mr. Tomorrow's judgement, it was prudent to return to the school. The staff who greeted the van was able to get Matte to leave the van although he was displaying a measure of obstinacy. Torey on the other hand tried to follow Matt out of the van but was prevented from doing so by staff members. She then climbed over a couple rows of seat and made her way off through the back door.

Acting in an erratic fashion she began to run up and down the street eventually running into the middle of the street and sitting there as vehicles were forced to take evasive measures or come to a complete stop to avoid hitting her. The police were called, and she was detained. Apparently she was undergoing a mental health crisis which required her to be referred to a mental health center.

One evening as I was dropping students off, De'Cray and Waybill (another student) got into a verbal altercation on the van. As they continued with their verbal back and forth, the rhetoric escalated to the realm of threats. Waybill was sitting in the front passenger seat and everything about his body language, buttressed by his tone of voice, suggested he was preparing to fight. De'Cray was sitting in the row directly behind the driver's seat, and he too, was preparing for a brawl. I observed the female passenger who was seated next to De' Cray putting her arm around him in an effort to restrain and keep him calm.

The disputants were both wearing their seatbelts, and I was able to convince them to stay buckled in. We were then approaching Waybill's house, and he swore he was going to fight De' Cray when we got to his stop. As we pulled up to his gate, he unbuckled his seatbelt, jumped out of the van, pulled open the rear passenger door, pushed past the female student that was sitting between De' Cray and the rear passenger door and jumped on De' Cray who instantly held him in a headlock. All of this happened so quickly, and I had to physically intervene to help release the grip that De' Cray had on Waybill's neck.

At that point Waybill continued making threats and took off running into his house with the promise of returning to the van with a weapon. I quickly closed the rear passenger door, got back in the driver's seat and drove off. The next stop was De' Cray's, and while driving to that destination, Waybill called De' Cray's cell phone. From what I could tell, the conversation was one of reconciling their dispute and I was happy for that. However, I was not going to forgo the necessary step of holding them accountable for their actions on the van. I wrote them both up and recommended that neither of them returned to school unless accompanied by a parent or guardian. By the time they returned, there did not seem to be any 'beef' between the two, so apparently they reconciled on their own. In the following days, De' Cray had a number of consecutive absences.

CHAPTER FOUR

Worried By Absences

Consecutive and extended periods of absence are usually a concern for staff, for we are not able to provide supervision of the youths in those circumstances, and bad things have happened under these conditions. Oftentimes parents and guardians are not in a position to supervise either. They have their own commitments to attend to; going to their jobs for example. In addition, parents or not, youths may be left to their own devices so the temptation is there for a youth to exploit his freedom with less than positive outcomes. These could include the youth being arrested as a result of a pick-up order, the commission of a crime by the youth or even a youth succumbing to a gunshot wound. In De' Cray's case, he was incarcerated for shooting and killing another youth. His future at this point is uncertain. *A recent update on the news is that De' Cray turned eighteen years old and the case was tried. He has been given a sentence of thirty-five years in prison.*

I could recount at least three other cases of death of a youth who stopped attending school. In a conversation with a former teacher who had done this type of work for more years than I had, I learned that that teacher had lost sixteen students over the years. It runs counter to any kind of logic and represents an indictment upon a society in which this type of devaluation of human life is allowed to perpetuate. Note that these accounts are only a microcosm of a microcosm of a microcosm of a crisis that seems unworthy of addressing with even the most miniscule of urgency. For those who think that this maelstrom is localized, or confined to one expendable strata of society, I implore you to think again. It cannot be a benefit to society at large if a whole generation of young people is lost to either prison or the grave.

It could be a little taxing to assign blame, for the subjectivity of a simple finger-pointing exercise might miss the mark by far. Sociologists are invited to drill down on my thesis here to either eschew or further crystallize my thought process, but I could confidently say from my point-of-view that this situation stinks. As I continue to enumerate the instances of deadly violence suffered by some of my students, there was the case of Jawan who got shot in the back of his head, execution style, while on the basketball court.

He was a youth who loved to talk about goings on in his neighborhood and society at large. I once asked him whether he was in any way phased by the acts of violence that routinely occur in his neighborhood. He informed me that the instances of violence have become so commonplace that he was not worried about it in the least. He went on to say that he has witnessed people being shot and falling dead in the street. Jawan was a very vocal youth whose voice was silenced forever. He was just another one caught up in the tangled, no-way-out web of gang affiliation.

It is a state of affairs which leads a youth to express that there is something known as a '21 Club' in their world. Antonio educated me about this one day after class. When I asked him to explain what '21 Club' meant, he told me that many young people, he included, were of the belief that if they made it to their 21st birthday, they stood a chance of living a long life. If you are reading this and your reaction is "Oh my God!" or "Unbelievable!" while your stomach churns, then declare yourself to be a living, feeling human being. If you feel apathetic, then your heart was redone with concrete.

Taye was another one who stopped attending regularly. One evening I saw on the news where he was shot and killed, and the police and his relatives were appealing to the public for information that would lead to the arrest of his killer. The killer had still not been caught during the weeks and months following his death, and I need not go into the unfortunate state of distrust between certain communities and the police. Suffice it to say that if the situation was different, many murders would have been solved and a reasonable potential for the reduction in youth-on-youth crime might have emerged.

What we see instead is the willingness of rivals to seek their own deadly retribution which in turn unleashes a cascade of revenge killings; making victims of guilty and innocents alike. The effect of this is perpetual squabbles and an expansion of the membership of the '21 Club'. In response to my question about when all of this mayhem will end, I have even had a youth offer the heart-wrenching opinion that he believes there is no end in sight. *(Think for a moment what this means for urban communities in particular and America as a whole. Weigh the benefits and the costs. Weigh the social and economic costs. Weigh the psychological pain. Weigh the engendered fears; justified or not).*

My point is that none of us should entertain the misguided notion that these events are occurring outside of our comfort zones so we need not pay attention. I do not have a crystal ball, but I have a hunch that in a nation that is so steeped in violence, this type of violence among young people will straddle all ethnicities and sectors in this nation. Sufficient to mention here would be the well-known fact that mass killings tend to occur in the suburbs, and most of the perpetrators of these killings do not come from the *'hood'*.

I will move past the debate about access to guns in this country because commonsense is a scarce commodity in this regard. Taye was always sleepy in class and showed no particular inclination to do his classwork. That behavior too, is contraindicative to a state of wellbeing or wholeness of self, and to an observant and caring teacher, it might appear as a cry for help, a display of a sense of resignation that the youth feels inside, or a tacit clue that the youth may be thinking he has reached the zenith of his life and is prepared to deal with *whatever.*

A sad case involving three former students made the news. The news reported that one of the students was killed. Following that event, there was a somber atmosphere at the school seeing that the student who died had just exited the program. The staff seemed to have been more deeply affected by the incident than the students were; perhaps the students had become a little numb to experiences like these. Unofficial accounts of the incident suggested that the students conspired to invite a drug dealer over to one of their houses with the intention of robbing him of his drugs and money. When he arrived, some sort of altercation blew up leading to gunfire that left one of the students dead.

CHAPTER FIVE

MIAMI VICES

Billy was a youth who would present with a similar sense of resignation as Taye. The only difference was that he did not appear to be sleepy all of the time, and he was open to building a relationship with at least one staff member – Miss Tanny. She was the only one that he would halfway reach out to. I don't think she learned a lot about him, but I suspect he had a teenage crush on her, and I believe she knew it too. There may not be much value in my next statement, or maybe there is in a cosmic kind of way, but I just wanted to mention that Miss Tanny was a Caucasian lady and Billy was a bi-racial male with a Caucasian mother and an African-American father.

I knew as much that his father was not in his life and was somewhere doing life or an extensive prison sentence. Billy did not speak much, but he wrote poems. He seemed to be a rather introspective youth oblivious to his surroundings. He would also do some of the class assignments but only grudgingly. I concluded that he knew how to do the work but was quietly refusing to conform to a system of academic rules which demanded his compliance and threatened his freewill to be part of it or not be part of it. This was speculation on my part, but I totally got it. In some respects, my own thinking resonates with a radical posture that can see through fluff and separate it from something that truly caters to my ambitions and visions for maximal achievement.

For some people, achievements are not always academic in nature, but from my perspective, it is worth the effort to build at least a reasonable academic foundation upon which every other life pursuit can rest. A carpenter or plumber will still need to be able to interpret the distances he measures with his construction tape in order to align item A with item B. Higher academic pursuits are indicated for professions requiring the engagement of expanded intellectual faculties, but melded together, it is the skill of the tradesman along with the skill of the university graduate that helps make society work.

One morning we received the news that Billy was shot and killed in a Miami park. The report said that he was sitting on a park bench and a shooting erupted between rival gangs of youths. Billy was unfortunately struck in the head by a bullet intended for someone else. The news saddened us, but appeared to strike Ms. Tanny especially hard. Ms. Tanny was the mother of a bi-racial son so, upon reflection, her affinity for Billy could have been that she saw him as if he were her own son because her son and Billy were part of the same racial component ; mixed between a Caucasian mother and an African-American father – both fathers being of Jamaican heritage. Ms. Tanny framed one of Billy's poems and hanged it on her classroom wall as a tribute to him.

Frank was sixteen years old at the time. He was a student who would argue any point and provide his type of logic to support it. Although his logic could sometimes seem illogical, he stuck to his point and would probably be able to prevail if he was presenting a legal argument. I was certain he had the temperament and curiosity of mind to pursue legal studies, but there was a struggle between that career potential and a lifestyle that was more likely to land him on the other side of the law. He was difficult to deal with when he was in his troubled state, but I built a relationship with him that allowed me to approach him sometimes when other staff members could not.

Frank and I both had shaved heads, so I would stand next to him and declare how we look alike. One particular day he was really in his feelings; cursing out everybody and throwing things across the room. I stood next to him and said, "son what's wrong?" He replied, "I am not your son"! Then I said, "How do you know, don't you see how much we look alike"? I took the chance to take the conversation to that level hoping that he would find it funny and change his mood. To my surprise he took the bait and started smiling. At that point I put my arm around him, and told him everything would be alright. We were all thankful at the school because he was calm for the rest of the day. Unfortunately, months later, I saw on the news from Miami where he had shot and killed his girlfriend because she cheated on him.

Obando was part of the LGBTQ+ community and, at eighteen years old, was preparing to exit the program. He was in the process of transitioning from male to female and had developed a more feminine appearance, particularly in his chest, which he attributed to hormone therapy. However, he mentioned that he had not yet been able to afford surgery for his lower anatomy. Obando was very open about his life outside of school, often discussing his work as a sex worker. According to him, many of his clients were professionals or community leaders, most of whom were married.

What made Obando particularly notable was his fearless attitude. He wouldn't back down from any student who challenged him, and he was more than willing to escalate beyond a verbal confrontation if necessary. The other students were well aware of this and treated him with a level of respect, knowing full well not to provoke him.

Reflecting on Obando reminds me of Alicen, a student from another alternative school. While Alicen never explicitly stated his gender identity, he often wore a bra and fishnet stockings to school. He frequently spoke about being in an abusive relationship with a teenage boy, while also expressing his feelings for a girl he deeply cared for. Alicen had gone all out preparing for a date with her, searching for an elegant dress and making reservations at a classy restaurant. However, he was devastated when the girl changed her mind, leaving him heartbroken after all the effort he had put into the evening.

Much like Obando, Alicen had a reputation among his classmates as someone they didn't want to cross. His peers sensed an intimidating presence about him, which made them cautious in their interactions.

Sometimes students would come to school and it would be obvious that they are overwhelmed by some sort of internal struggle. They could either express their frustration by lashing out at staff or other students or they would simply recoil within themselves and look pensive throughout the day. The staff routinely participates in professional development activities including learning about mental health concerns and alerting us to signs to look for when a student is undergoing a crisis. These trainings are valuable because they help staff members to realize that many of the verbal aggressions students display towards them are not personal and have little to do with the staff member who is subjected to that aggression.

For a teacher, the loss of a student is equivalent to the loss of a family member, because so much of the adult/ youth interaction happens at school between the hours of 8 or 9am and 4 or 5pm in the case of youths who attend alternative day programs. What happens outside of these hours is always concerning for staff as mentioned above. We always hope that the positive experience we give them during the school day will carry over to the intervening hours before we see them again. The reality is, however, that there are forces beyond our control that threaten to undo the daily input we make into their lives. So it is usually a good thing when we see them showing up to school.

School has a considerable degree of value for the students as well. Even if they are not too excited by the academic part, they love being at a place where they could have fun and socialize with each other. The academic work was not particularly difficult, and all of them came to us because the Court referred them to our school. Many have been out of regular school for months and even years. It is not necessarily laudable to have an eighteen-year-old youth assigned to the seventh grade, a seventeen-year-old to the ninth grade or a sixteen-year-old to the sixth grade.

With all of the wrong turns these youths have made in their lives, they were now faced with the reality that a successful future demands that they reconfigure their focus. Not many of them intended to go back to regular school after completing our program, so they chose the GED option instead. This option requires the requisite amount of studying, but some of these youths struggled with remaining committed enough to bring themselves up to that level of preparedness. However, we continued to encourage them to stay the course.

CHAPTER 6

MICKEY & TYER'S WORLD

At this juncture, I will make mention of two students, Mickey and Tyer, who had passed three of the four subjects necessary to obtain the GED certificate. Both appeared to display intermittent interest in passing the test and both appeared to do so for different reasons. Mickey, without a shadow of a doubt, was more than capable of passing, but his interest was not consistently observable. There were times when he would come to school and show no appetite for academic work. On the few occasions when he would participate, he would either Christmas tree an assignment, or on a rare occasion he would take the time to do the assignment well.

There was a general feeling among the staff that he underperformed in his first GED test on purpose. Working with these youths as long as we have, we came to get a sense of what might possibly be underlying some of their seeming reticence regarding personal success. It was the second time in the program for Mickey. He was with us two years prior, and had been back for a few months after committing some offence in the interim.

Passing all of his GED subjects would have meant summarily departing the program successfully, and in my interactions with him, it appeared he did not necessarily look forward to leaving an acquired family atmosphere and going back to the drudgery of a life where he had an estranged, drug-using mother and an absent father. He lived with his mother's ex-boyfriend and his two daughters and those girls presented a source of stress with their lack of attention to cleanliness and interest in school. Mickey felt pressured to be the girls' guide, but they never seemed to listen to him.

He worked at a fast food place after school, and after he will have passed his GED he intended to try, after months of staff encouragement, to join the United States Navy. Mickey has on several occasions, got set to fight other youths, and had been a behavior issue because of his petulant moods. I jokingly told him that the annoyance that his sisters presented to him was karma for the annoyance he presented the staff with. He missed a passing grade on his last GED test by one point, and after that, he seemed a little more motivated to get it over with. A lot was riding on that test result because he was just a few months shy of his eighteenth birthday.

He had been struggling with drug use, and it was hoped that an opportunity to go to the navy would put him on a good path for what would seem to be the first time in his life. Mickey was the kid with whom I have had perhaps the best rapport at the school, and I had never counted him out because I knew his potential even if he may not have allowed himself to see what I saw in him, as clearly as I have. The main thing I wanted him to know was that he was worthy and capable of moving from a mindset of hopelessness to one of hopefulness.

I had told him that he looked like a young Clint Eastwood, and a movie gig might even be available to him one day. He had already proven that he liked drama; once coming to school with hickeys all over his face and neck apparently due to an amorous encounter, with two older females, that got a little intense. Mickey accidentally shot off one of his fingers while playing with a gun, and had been hospitalized for getting into a car accident in which he was almost tossed through the windshield.

In the latter case, he was not the driver, but got into a physical altercation with the driver while the car was in motion. Mickey has been known to make some decisions that boggle the mind. Once after purchasing a bicycle at a store, he decided to ride the bike instead of walking it out of the store. Well, his foot got caught in the spokes of the bike's wheel and he fell off the bike fracturing his ankle. He had been known to sneak into a room where there were snacks and, without permission, help himself to the items. The staff would sometimes discover this after the fact.

I would famously tell him that he was a fairly smart but a really dumb kid. I would also tell him that I was tempted to call him 'sticky fingers' but with only nine fingers, that label would miss the mark by one digit. As I mentioned, he and I had a good relationship, so he knew that no harm was intended by any of the above comments. Mickey stayed in touch with me through Facebook, and would update me on his status in life. As far as I could tell, he still works at a fast food place, has not obtained his GED certificate, and didn't pursue the Navy option.

Tyer is another youth that I had a good relationship with, but I knew when to approach him and when not to approach him. He was a kind of complicated figure, and the staff knew this. I had opined that the devil walked with Tyer in the mornings. I had never seen a young man so grumpy, disrespectful and disregarding of program requirements as he. It is to be noted that he surprised us on occasion by reversing the order of his eccentric portrayals. In those instances he would come in, put his head down, and refuse to talk to anyone. Later in the day however, he would awaken with cursing out staff, cursing out 'imaginary' rivals, cursing out circumstances that he says he didn't want to talk about, and being disruptive in class.

He had a disheveled appearance and persona. Staff knew to be ready to supply him with a pair of shoes and pants in order for him to look more appropriate for class. He would normally complain about these items and vocalize his desire to go back home. After being searched, youths would assemble in Large Group to eat breakfast. Quite often, Tyer would continue his diatribe of complaints as he unbridled his suite- of -misery; much to the annoyance of multiple pairs of ears in Large Group and beyond.

When he got to class,, he would sometimes put his head down and carry on with his verbal assaults on subjects human and inanimate, and continue this way until he is written up for profanity and disruption. In this case, he would be taken out of class to do consequences commensurate with his offenses. This could mean cleaning, taking out trash or being put in ISS (In-School Suspension). It should be noted that cleaning to Tyer is a welcome gesture, for when he would be free from the grip of his apparent demons he would volunteer to clean the classrooms and take out the trash.

This situation normally presented itself at the end of the day on days when his seeming 'exorcism' took place. One notable Friday was a good day for Tyer. He came to school disheveled in appearance but sober in mind. He still had to be given a pair of pants and shoes, but his mood was docile instead of disturbed. He hardly spoke throughout the morning, but broke his silence to do his class assignments including reading an entire story about Aliens and UFOs to the class.

Taking the initiative to read was not unusual for him. This was what he did, but usually during the last class period of the day. He did it in the morning on the Friday in question, and I admired that because new students were able to witness it and hopefully be inspired to do likewise in the days ahead. Tyer's living situation is a source of stress for him, but unlike Mickey's, his neighborhood is not a peaceful place. He would talk about the shootings and violence that were all too common.

As I mentioned before, he and I had a good rapport and he would let me in on some of the goings on in his area of town. He was sometimes one of the youths on my drop-off route, and I had noticed on top of some of the telephone poles in his neighborhood there are police lights and cameras. When I asked what those were for, another student explained that they were 'shot spotters'. A 'shot spotter' I learned, is a way to trace where gunfire was coming from so that the police could pinpoint and investigate that spot. His neighborhood was constantly under surveillance, but I suppose that is the era in which we live.

I think empathy is in order for so many of our kids who tend to be under siege in their own neighborhoods. They don't feel free to walk at night or even in certain blocks during daylight hours. They refer to the members of their rival gangs as 'opps', and 'opps' may live on the adjacent block. Tyer is not immune from this state of affairs because there are certain areas where he would not, or could not go. It is so unfortunate that these youths had been convinced by someone that the youth on the next block is their enemy. I tried to tell them that the youth on the next block is really their brother, but they had been so brainwashed that a whole generation of young men are wiping themselves out for the benefit of no one; at least not for the benefit of their families or those who love and care about them.

I remember during the first couple of weeks on my pick-up route the van fell low on gasoline. I informed the youths on the van of my intention to stop at a gas station. I started to pull over to the first gas station I saw, but one youth declared with disbelief in his voice, "Not here"! "Don't stop here"! I, being unaware of the reason why he reacted that way, asked him why I couldn't stop there. He explained that it was dangerous to do so on that block. As I look back on the situation, I want

to say that it was probably less for my safety than for his. This was long before I had any knowledge about what an 'opps' is and how dangerous it was for certain youths to be seen in certain neighborhoods.

I remember suggesting to Tyer one evening that I modify the order in which I did drop-offs a little bit and drop him off last because I wanted to speak with him while we drove. He said he was not prepared to do that unless I drove by his house so he could pick up his 'pole'(firearm) because he would not be seen in another area 'unstrapped'. Well, that became a non-starter so I dropped him off first as usual.

There was another instance when I was dropping off another student. It was nighttime and that time of year when Daylight Savings Time had already ended and darkness fell in the early evenings. The area was unfamiliar to me so the youth on the van was assisting me with directions. He was the last drop-off for that route. As we neared a block, there were some young men standing outside a house. Upon seeing them, my passenger ducked down placing his head in his lap and pulling his hoodie over his head. We passed that area without incident, and to my amazement, my passenger only lived a few houses around the corner from where the young men were standing. Just as Tyer had said before, this youth told me he took those evasive measures because he didn't have his 'pole' with him.

On another occasion when I was doing my drop-off rounds, one youth asked me to drop him off on the opposite side of the street so that it would be easier for me to continue the route. As he was preparing to exit the van, he looked up the street and announced that he had seen 'somebody' and that I should take him directly to his house. I complied with his request even though it meant making a U-turn.

Several miles away on the same drop-off route there was a major accident at an intersection. This meant that we would be considerably delayed trying to get the next youth to his house. His house was less than two hundred yards from the intersection, but the road to his house was temporarily blocked off. The best option was for him to walk the short distance home. He agreed to take up the challenge, but to my surprise, when he got off the van he broke out into a sprint towards his house. That act might appear strange to most people, but I had been sufficiently educated about the facts of hood life not to understand his decision.

In none of the cases I related did the youths seem to consider my safety as a paramount concern, I endeavored to drop the youths off at or near their doorsteps, but that was not always possible due to the distance between the parking lot and the youth's front door. For some of the youths who lived in middle class neighborhoods, I was able to pull up into their driveways. Some of their houses could be the envy of working class people, but the appearance of a house is not necessarily an indicator of the minds that dwell inside that house.

CHAPTER 7

SEARCHES

In the morning when the students get off of the van, they are subjected to searches of their persons then a staff member uses a wand to try to detect any objects that they might be concealing. When we open the door for them to enter the search area, they simply walk past the staff at the doorway without even an attempt to offer a 'good morning' greeting. And even when the staff member utters a salutary word, they would keep their eyes forward as if the staff member is not there. For me this is disrespect, but it seems as if it is just another aspect of cultural malaise.

I would say that in a high percentage of the time we would discover unauthorized items, but they still manage to get stuff past the search process. These cunning offenders find ways to transport disallowed items by hiding them in unreachable chambers in their undergarments. Luckily we had not discovered any potentially deadly weapons, but one time a search of a youth's backpack revealed a toy gun. The item looked like a real nine- millimeter weapon, and before determining that it was in fact fake, there was a period of consternation and anxiety by the staff member making the discovery.

On several occasions, not even a thorough search or the use of the wand could detect contraband that they are carrying on their persons, but there have been a number of instances where the classroom teachers discovered cell phones, cigarette lighters and vape cartridges after detecting suspicious interactions or body language by the youths. I can attest to examples of a youth appearing uncomfortable in his seat and standing up to adjust his pants, or a female putting her hands in her bosom with her face halfway submerged and her fingers moving under her sweater in a texting motion.

In those cases I would go over to the youth's location and simply say in a stern voice, "Give it to me"! The retort would usually be, "Give what to you, I don't have anything"! Then I would ask them to turn out their pockets or I would check their sweater sleeves. Or I would radio the behavioral staff to come and remove them from the classroom and search them again. Most of the time the student-suspect would hand the items over to me, and I would call or send a text message for behavioral staff to pick the items up.

One time as I was teaching the class, I saw a puff of smoke coming from the back of the room. I had to do a double take by shutting and opening my eyes again, and calling upon my brain to quickly process this strange phenomenon. Once my eyes, my brain, and I became convinced that I had really seen what I had seen, I sent a message for a staff to come to my classroom and get the item. This time Ms. Catherine, a case manager, came and retrieved the item and took the student away.

There was another incident like this one a few months later. This time I actually observed the student puff on the vape three times. When I asked him to hand it over he refused, saying he didn't have a vape. Even the students sitting next to him encouraged him to hand it over since he was caught red-handed, but he refused. I radioed for staff to come to my room, and Mr. Cobbler, Education Director, took the student out of class and retrieved the vape. I have to note that when we retrieve these items ungloved we immediately use hand sanitizer or wash our hands.

Clearly the items make it past searches hidden in areas proximate to the students' private parts, and cleanliness is not always attendant with this set of humans across the board. Many come to class without showering or bothering to brush their teeth, and are quite odoriferous when in close proximity to staff or other students. One of them even wore the same underwear all week and had no shame about donning sagging pants in accordance with the fashion standard of the day. I have had to employ discreet skills to draw attention to this situation with some of them. I kept a vial of cologne in my desk drawer and made it available to the ones who needed it.

It is almost gross to relate this next situation, but it makes the point concerning the ungloved protocol when retrieving contraband. One of the students who sneaked in a vape by way of his nether region was reported by some of the students to have shared that pipe with at least one other student during the school day. Later I heard some of the students say that they observed fecal stains on his underwear one time when he bent over to pick up a pencil from the floor. If nothing else makes the case for not sharing smoking paraphernalia, that has to be it, but even though I wish that these youths would stop bringing in vapes and attempting to smoke in class, it would be foolhardy of me to think that they would stop the practice even in light of the fact that they have to face consequences when caught.

Case Manager Ms. Minstrel observed a youth inhaling smoke from a vape cartridge while she was supervising the game room. She reported that when the youth saw that he had been caught, he tried to keep the smoke in his mouth in an effort to suggest that he did not inhale from the vape. Well, that was not as ingenious as he thought it would be, so he broke out into a coughing spell; expelling a mixture of sputum and smoke through his mouth. I make it a point often to try to encourage the youths not to engage in practices that would compromise their health. Vaping has been shown, scientifically, to damage the brains of adolescents.

The following are data published by The Centers for Disease Control.
1. A CDC study found that 99% of the e-cigarettes sold in assessed venues in the United States contained nicotine.[1]
2. Some vape product labels do not disclose that they contain nicotine, and some vape liquids marketed as containing 0% nicotine have been found to contain nicotine.
3. Nicotine can harm the developing adolescent brain. The brain keeps developing until about age 25.
4. Using nicotine in adolescence can harm the parts of the brain that control attention, learning, mood, and impulse control.[2]

One youth, John, does not miss an opportunity to debate the merits or folly of established norms; one time even debating that he should not be chastised for not sitting all the way up when Mr. Clelland, Behavior Modification Specialist, asked him not to continue lying down in his seat. John changed his posture from lying flat on the bench to a reclining position. Of course it is not comfortable sitting in a reclining position without back support, but John just wanted to put his act of defiance on display by offering the explanation that he responded to the request in the affirmative since he was no longer lying flat on the bench.

We all knew his temperament, so with a little coaxing, Mr. Clelland was able to get him to sit upright. Anyway, on the matter of vaping and young people, John suggested to me that vaping is an addiction for the ones who engage in it, and we, the school staff, should take that into consideration when deciding on consequences for the youths who sneak these items in and even smoke in class. He went on to draw the parallel with adults who smoke cigarettes knowing it is bad for their health. I asked him if he understood how smokers and their families suffer when this habit leads to lung cancer and other diseases, and how young people are exposing themselves to a life of poor health and the pains that come with it. I emphasized that it would not be good for society at large when its most vibrant sector consists of a high percentage of sufferers from diseases that wreak havoc on families.

John was a very smart young man, and it was always a pleasure conversing with him on the route home from school. We talked about international events, and at sixteen years old, he had a very good sense of history and the cause and effects of historical events. At times, however, he took to rapping, and the lyrics to some of the songs he sang —songs they all sang- are nothing short of conditioning for the pursuit of nothingness. I tried to tell them that the more they recite these gang-related, self-devaluing, life-cheapening lyrics, the more they will manifest this negativity in their lives.

John is a good example of the paradox that envelops his generation. They have a sense of right and wrong, but more easily embrace wrong sentiments. I must note here that paradoxes are found in every generation, but it seems to be more prevalent in this current generation: even with all of the advanced knowledge and easy access to information. The same access is also available to marketers who sometimes choose to peddle poison to the youths not for the advancement of the youths, but for the expansion of the art of profiteering. It is almost puke-inducing to hear some of my students talk about their preferences in vape flavors.

My take on John's perspective is that whereas I have some empathy for the addiction part, the rules of the school need to be obeyed. And taken into a fuller spectrum, non-addiction is preferable to addiction. Knowing John as I did, he was likely to come back with the cheeky remark that a life of non-addiction is an addiction in and of itself, so the possibility for infinite rhetoric was trending to be obvious in the discourse he and I were engaged in.

Septimus Barrock

CHAPTER 8

IN THE TRAP

Do you remember the two riders on the van when we went to pick up Roland for school? Well one day, one of them, Matt, made the declaration in a casual conversation that his life's ambition was to own a number of trap houses. One cannot help but admire his penchant for entrepreneurship, but the illegal nature of his business vision will likely imperil him and render his pursuit dead on arrival. Or he, himself, could be dead on arrival at his place of business. For me, Matt's dream, if not completely original, smacks of a flirtation with originality; especially coming from a person as young as he was. And it engenders a degree of speculation on my part regarding the business model he would be benchmarking. Is it his intention to secure a franchise from an established merchandizing chain? Would that business chain be known as Trap Houses Are Us?

From what I have heard, there are in fact trap houses in neighborhoods around town, but I am not of the belief that there is a chain of them, so Matt might be on to something. For the uninitiated, a trap house is a place where drug dealers and prostitutes and their clients congregate. At least this is the way the students explained it to me. It is kind of like a low-end speakeasy of the illegal drug business; providing substandard illegal goods and services. Sometimes the students will point out suspected trap houses to me, and even suggest that there are some familiar, drug-addicted young people who frequent those places.

Months after Matt left the school I gave him a random call to see how he was doing. He did not seem to be up to much at that stage of his life, but he said he was not in the trap house business, and did not seem to be in any legitimate money-earning business either. Giving a call to follow up on a youth's progress was not unusual for the staff. Sometimes we got reports that the youths have had steady employment, fathered or mothered babies, been incarcerated, gone back to regular school, or just chillin' with no particular focus or ambition.

Antonio has contacted me on a couple of occasions since he left; the most recent being a few weeks ago. He was happy to report that he is gainfully employed and staying focused. We reminisced on his time at the program and some of his cohorts when he was there. He and Mickey got along well, but they did not stay in touch after Antonio left. He wanted to know how Mickey was doing, and I updated him on Mickey's return to the program and his progress regarding his GED efforts. I am not surprised that Antonio has stayed out of trouble after leaving because he always impressed me as someone who had a measure of ambition.

When he was at the program, he would tell me about a girl he regarded as his best friend, and he was also in love with her but did not have the courage to tell her. He told me he had dreams of moving to California with her to pursue a career in entertainment. All of this was contingent upon her willingness to travel this life path with him, but he never made her aware of his thinking. She moved to North Carolina with her relatives, and he subsequently moved to South Carolina with his relatives. He never met up with her in the Carolinas. He is back in Florida, while she is still in North Carolina. They do not correspond anymore because the friendship has waned due to distance, or lack of interest on her part, or maybe as he suggests, she found a boyfriend in North Carolina.

Sometimes students came back to visit us to bring us up to date with their progress in life. Two sisters dropped by dressed in their medical scrubs to touch base with Mr. Cobbler and other staff that left after the sisters completed the program. It so happened that they were not able to see any of the staff members in question, and Mr. Cobbler was off on that day. They promised to come back another time. On a couple of occasions, female past students have shown up with their babies to show us what they have been up to since they left the program. There is no lack of encouragement by the staff for students to choose options that could enhance the substance of their lives, but the staff is aware that the ultimate choice rests with the students themselves. Making babies at such a young age is not one of the streams of encouragement we give to them.

I would say that children are a blessing for those fortunate enough to have them or for those who choose to have them. Children, however, rank at the highest level of the demand curve, and their upkeep is so much more boosted when there are responsible adults in their lives. When these young girls have babies where the fathers are either locked up, or do not have a job, or are simply absent from the child's life, it robs the young child of so much. The girl is left to struggle by herself, or if she is lucky, the burden is unfairly passed on to the adults in the family. I have seen girls with two children at the age of sixteen, where the children's fathers are serving long prison sentences. One such case involved one of my students.

CHAPTER 9

THE GEENIE CHRONICLES

Geenie was a mother two times over, but Geenie, at sixteen years old, was also a child. I often say that these youths have seen too much and done too much at too young an age. They seem to have gone directly from infancy to adulthood in a moment of time, and there is a persistent struggle between a force that tries to keep them in the child zone and a force that tries to push them into the adult zone. Imagine being pulled in two opposing directions day in, day out, week in, week out, month in, month out, year in, year out and you are still a child! There is also a high likelihood that the children of these children are being modeled on this same cyclical template. At least with adults crossroads are also a reality, but adults are endowed with sufficient psychological tools to navigate this often temporary dilemma.

Geenie had moments of adultness when she would school her peers about their immature behaviors. She would encourage them to stop the excessive talking in class and to focus on doing their assignments. She was very good at staying on task and asking questions for clarification. She was a little-below-average student who had not attended regular school for quite some time, but she quickly caught on to concepts once they were explained to her. Some days she would come to class feeling sleepy and do part of the classwork before putting her head down on the desk. Even during the instances when she would be lethargic, she would promise to complete the assignments at a later time.

On other days, Geenie would engage her classmates in conversations about happenings in the neighborhood and amorous encounters she has had. I was able to conclude from overhearing one of her pronouncements that she had ambitions of becoming a stripper. In one of her conversations she mentioned how an acquaintance is into strip dancing, and there is a lot of money to be made in that industry. I was hopeful that she would consider alternative fields of endeavor, but I am aware she will make the choice that she is most drawn to. I have no particular inclination to look down on Geenie for wanting to consider stripping as a vocation because I know there are females more economically stable and more educated than she who are working in that field. During my time as a college professor, I had knowledge of at least two students who worked in that industry. Both went on to earn college degrees and all things being equal, both are likely employed in other, less salacious fields of endeavor.

When teenage students get involved romantically with a peer, there is more often than not a degree of toxicity; probably attributable to the undercurrents of immaturity that is still endemic to these teenage relationships. Geenie had at least a couple of relationships with fellow students. First it was Keenan, a younger male who talked a really smooth game, but seemed rather ill-prepared to handle a 'veteran' like Geenie. In a matter of a couple of weeks, their relationship went from signs of fawning to displays of physical aggression.

One morning as the students gathered in Large Group for breakfast, an argument erupted between Geenie and Keenan. As things escalated, Geenie walked over to Keenan's location and hit him over the head with a small milk carton. Keenan got up from his seat and attempted to strike her, but he was restrained by a staff member. Their animosity went on for a period of time until Geenie and Asta started dating. From what I garnered, there was some kind of clash on the outside between Geenie's affiliates and Keenan's affiliates culminating in Geenie's house being shot up. . It was interesting to see how they reconciled without any friction occurring between Keenan and Asta.

Everything seemed to happen so fast. Geenie was a little younger than Asta and seemed to exhibit a genuine affection for him. Asta was someone who talked a lot about his encounters with rivals when he was locked up. He appeared to have some sort of reputation on the street, and none of the other youths at the school seemed to have had overt conflicts with him. It is a general theme (somewhat of a rite-of-passage) among teenage boys to talk about sexual conquests, real or imagined, as a way to boost their egos and remain pseudo-important in their circle of peers. It would normally not take long for a boy to let his peers know that he 'scored' with a girl in the school. He would even rate her performance during the encounter. And vice versa, a girl would rate a boy's performance. Nothing seemed to be sacred with these teenagers, and it is quite interesting to observe the way they treat the issue even though one should make provision for the fact that they are not 'mentally grown'.

Geenie and Asta continued their relationship for a considerable length of time until one day Asta was talking about physically attacking Geenie over some kind of love triangle situation. She would avoid sitting within proximity of him, and he made a couple of attempts to get at her but was prevented by staff from doing so. They had to be separated and monitored closely to avoid any clashes. The funny thing is that they rode the same van to and from school, and one day Ms. Blackstone, the van driver that morning, had to quell a tense argument between the two. That was the first sign a staff saw that something was awry between Asta and Geenie. During the period of malice between them, both would speak unflatteringly about each other, but at the same time talk to their classmates about how they missed each other. They were not in the same class, so this limited the opportunities for face-to-face contact.

There was a chance meeting between the two one time when the entire student body assembled. They relented on the bitterness and embraced the sweetness of each other's presence. They were in the love business once again and remained that way until Asta left the program followed a few weeks later by Geenie. A new youth, Fabio, entered the program during the last two weeks of Geenie's tenure, and word was that Fabio and Geenie had started a relationship and that the hickeys he had on his neck were the result of a passionate get-together with her on the outside. The status of their relationship was unknown at the time.

CHAPTER 10

OH MY'RA!

Keenan and Myra began dating. In keeping with his cougar preference, she had a couple of years on him. They would capitalize on any opportunity they could get to sit close to each other. They were not in the same class, but got to interact outdoors and in common areas. Possibilities for the display of affection were severely limited because students were always under the watchful eyes of peers and other staff. However, Keenan would, as boys do, report on his visits to Myra's house. He was a little more discreet than Asta regarding his conquest, but he still made it known to those who cared enough to observe.

Youths who have committed felonies are not supposed to associate with each other outside of school, but it is not possible for staff to be with them 24/7. We do daily curfew checks and regular home visits on youths who have had repeated absences from school, but it is also the responsibility of the guardians and the youths themselves to ensure the legal protocols are followed. Keenan and Myra remained an item for a short period of time. The novelty of the cougar/young buck affair wore off but not without its own quotient of drama. Myra had a caustic personality, and was known more for her disrespect to staff and peers alike. Most days she would do her classwork, but her anger would be triggered by just about anything. And so it was that she and Keenan got into a physical altercation ending their romantic relationship.

Enter Jeden! He fashioned himself as some sort of playboy outside of school, and had eyes on a couple of female students. He even opined that he could 'get' any of them he wanted. Jeden appeared to be more of a self-promoter than an actual Romeo, but he ended up in a relationship with Myra anyway. He was also a couple of years younger than her, but she declared that he was more mature than the other boys at the school. She seemed to have a genuine caring disposition when it came to him, and he seemed to relish the fact that he was able to capture her heart. For some reason, Myra started to skip school on a regular and extended basis. This led her JPO to recommend a Pick-up Order on her. She was subsequently found to be in violation of her contract, but started to attend school once again in hopes that this would lessen her chances of being sent off to a higher level program. When everything was considered together, it turned out that she had no recourse to avoid going to a residential program.

During the process to decide on whether or not she would be placed elsewhere, Myra tried to show a softer side and improve her behavior at school, but her normal self could not allow her to sustain this performance, and so she would often resort to her modus operandi of expletives and general disrespect for staff. I was able to have a one-to-one talk with Myra one day, and she let me into some of the overwhelming stresses she has had to deal with all her life. The absence of caring adults in her life, having to take care of her basic needs, on her own, at a very young age, not feeling loved, and precarious living situations have all been circumstances leading up to the angry person she had become. While conversing, mostly listening to her, I asked her about her dreams and career goals. She said she would like to have a better life and work in the healthcare industry, perhaps as a dental hygienist.

Myra displayed academic potential, and I know she could achieve her goal once she could clearly see the pathway that would take her there. With the reality that she was going away being front and center, her relationship with Jeden became a bit complicated. During one of my planning periods, they both asked to come to my classroom; not necessarily to talk with me, but so that they could have a non-judgmental space where they could talk things over. I was a little taken aback to see Myra weeping bitterly and expressing her fears that Jeden would 'hook-up' with Geenie once Myra was gone. The insecurity was palpable, and the weeping seemed intermittently inconsolable. Jeden turned to me and asked me to reassure Myra that Geenie was just his 'dawg' and she had nothing to worry about in that regard. I had a sense that Jeden and Geenie were just friends because I had never seen nor heard any suggestion that the two were a possible item. In any event, I did not offer an opinion in response to Jeden's' request, and from what I could tell, Geenie and

Myra were good friends. The Jeden/Myra episode occurred while Geenie was still at the school, but none of the fears expressed by Myra appeared to have reached Geenie's ears. The gossip channels did not seem to contain anything related to that matter.

After Myra's departure, Jeden seemed to have concentrated on relationships outside of the school until a new batch of students, including Rena, arrived. Rena presented as being a naive young girl but swore that most people view her as wise beyond her years. I encouraged her, just as I would all of the students, to remain focused and successfully complete the program while preparing for a future of realized goals and dreams. I suggested to her that she should not allow herself to be distracted by any of the boys in the program, and warned her that there is a culture among young boys where they report and even exaggerate on any romantic happenstance between them and any girl in the program. She said she understood, but she also knew that 'boys will be boys'.

Rena expressed to me that no one in her family had ever gone to college and she would like to be the first. In my view, she had the ability to achieve this goal, but her conviction to remain focused is somewhat tepid. Some students have a preference when it comes to communicating with individual staff members, and Rena has made it known that I am the staff member she is most comfortable communicating with. In response to my admonition that she stays focused and not allow herself to be distracted by any of the boys, she said that she knows what I am telling her is right, but as young people do, she would likely act in accordance with her feelings. It was semi-devastating to hear this, and the most I could hope for was that she would somehow be a little more introspective before acting, impulsively, on her feelings.

Jeden was on his way out; taking his last GED test and spending his last week in the program. During this time, Rena got word that Mera, a second-time enrollee, had expressed her interest in Jeden. This information was out in the open before Mera went off to a program and while Rena was not yet enrolled. Rena learned of the situation upon Mera's return and this made her sad indeed. There was talk about a possible fight occurring between Mera and Rena over Jeden. The gossip channel revealed that even though there had been mutual admiration between Mera and Jeden, noting of a romantic nature had ever occurred between them. Rena once intimated to me that of all the boys in the program, Jeden impressed her as being the most mature. Perhaps on the strength of this perceived maturity, Rena thought it prudent to 'act on her feelings' and become a romantic item with him, even consummating the relationship in a matter of days. I learned of this on the Monday of the week that Jeden left the program.

It was customary for me, on a Monday, to ask random students about their weekend. And so Jeden, in the presence of Rena, divulged that "I was in her over the weekend". I later asked her about what he had said, and she confirmed that they had had a sexual encounter but it was not supposed to happen. According to her, it happened because the opportunity was there, and she did not control her feelings. In subsequent days, she had fears of missing her period, but it finally came after being delayed by a couple of days. Needless to say, I continued to encourage her to think about possible consequences of her actions before acting on impulses. I know that female staff members have offered her counseling as well.

CHAPTER 11

THE WRONG PATH

It is quite concerning for caring adults in instances where we could clearly recognize when young people are going down the wrong path and feel helpless as they pursue that path anyway. It is too often in the teenage years when one bad choice could completely change the course of a person's life. I must observe, however, that the maturity adults enjoy has resulted from years of mental and psychological growth, and even from trial and error. Survival in some circumstances could sometimes even be attributable to pure luck. I can recall risk-taking activities that some of my childhood friends and I have been involved with, and not every one of us came out of those activities alive.

One childhood friend dove off of an elevated position onto some rocks that lay just below the surface of the water and died of the head injuries he suffered. We would normally dive off that rock when we went to the beach, but on that day the tide was low and my friend did not think the situation through before making the dive. I also remember being in a car with a friend who thought it was a really fun thing to do to overtake another vehicle at a blind corner. A blind corner is a street configuration where a driver is not able to see the traffic coming from the other direction because the roadway is constructed at a near ninety degree angle, and there are physical features blocking his view. *As I make mention of the term 'blind corner' here, I recall a joke involving a feeble old man who was so nervous about driving around one of those corners that he got out of his vehicle, shuffled to a point where he could verify that there was nothing coming in the opposite direction, shuffled back, got into his vehicle, and by the time he drove off, he collided with a car traveling in the other direction.* Fortunately for us, just when we completed the turn, we missed a truck by inches.

I always reflect on the saying that 'youth is wasted on the young', and I would tell my students about this regularly. The lesson presented by the saying is that when a person is young, has youth, he has all of the energy but not the maturity. However when a person is older, he has the maturity but not the quota of energy possessed by young people. I suppose nature did not find it expedient to simultaneously install both assets in every individual. Or maybe it was a deliberate act of nature to demand temperance and humility, and make us learn lessons to help us reflect and project with the gradual acquisition of more life tools. The youthful years are full of fun and excitement, and to the extent that a young person is physically and mentally fit to enjoy those years, he is almost guaranteed a taste of heaven when his indulgences are of a balanced nature, but he is also almost guaranteed a taste of hell when his indulgences are excessive and good sense is avoided.

For some, the wrong path may seem like the only path. Throughout this text, I have highlighted various episodes where characters find themselves in states of desperation and vulnerability. It takes discipline to chart a course toward progress, but for those unfamiliar with discipline as a guiding principle, it can feel like a game of whack-a-mole, where opportunities for a better future seem available to everyone but them. The temptation to take the easier path often leads to more hardship, but at certain moments, it can appear to be the only option. The outcome is an unwitting sacrifice of one's freedom and dignity.

Empathy becomes crucial in understanding the choices made by youths whose living circumstances demand immediate action—actions that, under different conditions, a rational person would approach more thoughtfully. However, there's a disconnection between these youths' mental and emotional development and the maturity required to navigate the complex realities they face every day. It's akin to asking a fourth-grader to solve high school-level math problems without having learned the foundational steps—yet expecting them to do so for their very survival.

TUG-O-WAR TEENS

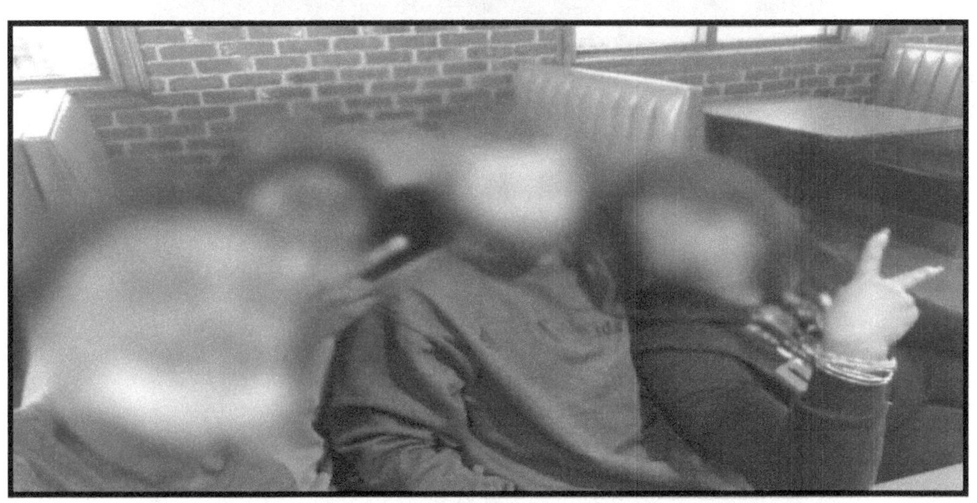

Every effort has been made to expose the students to positive opportunities and activities. Whether it was going on fishing trips, volunteering at community centers, visiting work sites, or participating in vocational courses, the students were placed in environments where they could benefit themselves and contribute to others. Some students volunteered at food banks, helping local residents in need of supplies, while others had the chance to assist at city golf tournaments.

On the vocational side, some students participated in scuba diving trips, where they earned their scuba diving credentials. Others became certified lifeguards, earned certificates in construction, or obtained TWIC badges, allowing them to work on ships. Additionally, many students completed their OSHA and Safe Staff certifications, enabling them to operate safely in the workplace. They were also given the opportunity to earn CPR and First Aid credentials, equipping them with critical life-saving skills.

The opportunities outlined above placed some of the students in unfamiliar situations, but they also gave them a sense of pride in completing these trainings. For many, a scuba diving trip was far removed from their daily routines, and hearing them excitedly talk about donning scuba gear and encountering marine life in the open ocean was something special. One can only hope that these experiences not only foster a sense of accomplishment but also open their eyes to possibilities beyond the limits of their everyday lives.

Incentives were built into the program to reward good behavior and encourage students to follow the rules and exceed expectations. One such incentive was the Bid Store, where students could redeem points they had earned for various items. While most of the inventory consisted of snacks and drinks, occasionally, more significant items like clothing, shoes, and even a TV were available. There was also a special chair in the cafeteria reserved for the student who scored the most points that week. It was remarkable to see how a student struggling academically or behaviorally could suddenly rise to become the "top dog" when properly motivated.

Staff always celebrated students' achievements and encouraged them to refocus when they slipped up. Mistakes were not uncommon, as many of the students were unaccustomed to experiencing success. It was as though they found themselves in a state of "comfortable discomfort," unable to fully trust in their ability to sustain progress. As a result, a student might earn a gold card one week, only to earn a blue or white card the next. A blue card, while not negative, signifies that the student is meeting, but not exceeding, expectations. During my time at the school, I observed that about three students left the program in a short period, largely due to their consistent success in earning gold cards, showing that they had learned to maintain excellence.

Thanksgiving was a particularly special time when donors, families, students, and staff gathered for a festive luncheon. It provided an opportunity to meet and connect in an atmosphere of camaraderie. On this day, the usual volatility seen in students' daily behaviors seemed to fade, replaced by the warmth of the Thanksgiving spirit. The scent and abundance of good food created a welcoming atmosphere, calming both stomachs and souls. Some families even received turkeys as gifts, adding to the sense of generosity and celebration.

Thanksgiving is a special time when donors, families, students, and staff come together for a lavish luncheon. It's an opportunity to meet, greet, and celebrate in an atmosphere of camaraderie. On this occasion, the usual volatility that sometimes lies beneath the surface of students' daily behavior seems to disappear, replaced by the warmth of the Thanksgiving spirit. The scent of good food fills the air, providing a sense of welcome and calm for both the body and the soul. Some families even receive turkeys as gifts, adding to the atmosphere of generosity and celebration.

Christmas is another time when students are especially happy to be part of the program. A Christmas Store is set up where students can choose items based on the points they've earned through compliance with the program's rules. The gifts are significant, ranging from clothing and shoes to games, TVs, and other valuable items. Since the program runs year-round, only the students who are still enrolled during the holiday season benefit from this festive reward. However, all students have the opportunity to be recognized and rewarded for their positive behavior whenever they are in the program.

CHAPTER 12

STAYING IN TOUCH

This past week, I heard from four of my former students. Tory sent me a message to let me know she's enrolled in prerequisite courses for her nursing studies while running a landscaping business on the weekends. Antonio called to share that he's been in a stable job for the past six months, and his prospects for growth within the company look promising. Sean and Rena FaceTimed me to catch up and reminisce about their time at the school. Rena is now a senior in high school and managing a part-time job, while Sean has been holding down the same job for the past two years.

In these conversations, I also learn about some students who are struggling. A few have unfortunately fallen into drug addiction, while others continue to have run-ins with the law. Staying in touch provides an opportunity to offer encouragement and guidance, reminding them to stay on a positive path. However, there are times when a student may reach out for financial help. While it's important to offer support where possible, there's always the concern of being taken advantage of. Vigilance, temperance, and professionalism are essential when communicating with former students. The genuine desire to see them succeed must remain the focus, even though their environment may not always be conducive to achieving that success.

EPILOGUE

In the chaos of these young lives—surrounded by crime, uncertainty, and societal disregard—there still remains a flicker of hope. It is not always easy to see, and for some, the path forward may feel impossibly blocked, but hope continues to exist in the small victories: a student completing their GED, another securing a stable job, or simply staying out of trouble long enough to glimpse a future they never imagined.

While not every story ends with redemption, it is vital to recognize the strength and resilience within these students, even when their environment seems designed to lead them astray. The opportunities we offer, the support we provide, and the encouragement we give can serve as lifelines for those willing to grab hold. It is in the moments of connection—when a student shares their dreams, seeks guidance, or finds a reason to keep pushing forward—that we see the true potential these youths possess.

The world they face is harsh, but our refusal to give up on them creates a bridge toward a better tomorrow. Each step forward, no matter how small, carries the promise of a life transformed. And while we may not be able to save every student, those we do reach are living proof that hope, combined with opportunity and persistence, can break even the strongest chains of despair.